EDINBURGH'S LAST DAYS OF S'

by
W.A.C. Smith

One and a half miles into its journey and No. 60096 would have passed St Margaret's locomotive depot, an archaic establishment dating from the opening of the North British Railway and bisected by the East Coast main line. At its peak, at the time of nationalisation in 1948, it had an allocation of more than 200 locomotives, but was not, in fact, the home depot of 'Papyrus', this being at Haymarket on the northern approach to the city. By the date of this photograph, 23 April 1966, steam was very much in decline at St Margaret's as, apart from Black Five No. 45127 and class B1 4-6-0 No. 61347, both pictured here, only twenty steam locos were present. The previous week No. 61347 had worked the last ever train from Edinburgh to Lanark.

Text and photographs © W.A.C. Smith, 2003.
First published in the United Kingdom, 2003, by Stenlake Publishing.
Telephone / Fax: 01290 551122
Reprinted 2006
Printed by St Edmundsbury Press Ltd

ISBN 1 84033 276 X

In steam's declining days one of the few regular duties remaining was that of carriage pilots. On 21 August 1964 standard class 4 2-6-4T No. 80122 waited to leave Craigentinny carriage sidings with a set of empty coaches for Waverley, as a two car diesel multiple unit, forming the 3.40 p.m. from Musselburgh, rattled past. Craigentinny carriage sidings dated from 1913 and survive today as a traction depot.

INTRODUCTION

The horse-operated Edinburgh & Dalkeith Railway was opened in 1831 to carry coal from the Midlothian collieries to the city, passengers also being conveyed, and a branch into Leith was added in 1838. The North British Railway purchased the concern in 1845 and converted it to locomotive haulage the following year.

The North British Railway had been promoted in 1842 – following upon the opening of the Edinburgh & Glasgow Railway – to build an east coast route southwards from Edinburgh to Dunbar and Berwick, with English money providing much of the finances. This was opened on 18 June 1846. The Edinburgh terminal was known as North Bridge, but within a few weeks it had become a through station with the opening of a connecting line through Princes Street Gardens from the Edinburgh & Glasgow Railway at Haymarket. A third railway, the Edinburgh, Leith & Granton, followed and had its platforms at right angles to the North British station with a tunnel under the New Town (this station was replaced in 1868 by a branch line from Abbeyhill). Variously known as North Bridge, General and Canal Street, the name Waverley was given to the station upon completion in 1862 of an alternative route south via Hawick and Carlisle – the Waverley Route.

The opening of the Forth Bridge in 1890 brought a massive increase in traffic, requiring a major reconstruction of Waverley and quadrupling of the tracks through Princes Street Gardens to Haymarket and on to Saughton Junction where a new line to the north left the original route to the west. Waverley now had twenty-one platforms covering twenty-three acres, with half under glass, and handled more than 1,000 trains per day, these including some 350 suburban services. It received colour light signalling in the 1930s together with a public address system.

The Caledonian Railway had been opened throughout from Carlisle to Glasgow and Edinburgh on 15 February 1848. Despite promises of a fine Italianate structure, its terminus in the capital was a temporary affair at Lothian Road, from where a short extension was made in 1870 to a new station at Princes Street, but Princes Street Station was partially destroyed by fire twenty years later and a new station was brought into use during 1893. Conveniently situated at ground level at the west end of Princes Street, its classical styling in red sandstone was set off internally by carved woodwork, its seven platforms being covered by an 850 foot long roof. From 1903 it was flanked on the east side by the sumptuous Caledonian Hotel, rivalling the massive North British Hotel which had opened the previous year at the opposite end of Princes Street.

Under the Railway Grouping Act of 1923, the North British Railway became part of the London & North Eastern Railway while the Caledonian Railway went to the London, Midland & Scottish Railway. Upon Nationalisation in 1948 both formed part of the Scottish Region of British Railways. The Beeching Report of 1963 claimed an over capacity of railway facilities in Edinburgh, resulting in the closure of Princes Street Station on 6 September 1965, its trains being accommodated at Waverley. Steam traction within the Scottish Region ended on 1 May 1967 and on British Railways as a whole on 11 August 1968.

Although passenger trains from Waverley to Granton ceased as early as 1925, most of the city's quite extensive suburban network faded away between 1962 and 1967 – despite dieselisation in 1958 – and one can speculate as to the part played in this by difficulty of access to and from Waverley Station for intending travellers. Its sunken location means steeply inclined carriageways which are both inconvenient and unattractive. Furthermore, the Waverley steps present an almost insurmountable barrier to many, yet London Underground stations were being served by electric escalators and lifts as early as 1910. Even the advent of main line electric services over both the east and west coast routes, in 1991 and 1993 respectively, has failed to bring any improvements in access to one of the national rail network's busiest stations.

Towards the end of the nineteenth century, the Caledonian Railway had proposed an ambitious suburban line with a circular route through Leith and including an underground section below the city centre. Unfortunately, this scheme never came to fruition (apart from a small portion at Leith used only by freight trains) for, while the underground section might well have been closed by the 1960s, or earlier, as happened with its similar Glasgow Central Low Level line, part of the latter was electrified and reopened in 1979 to form a useful addition to the Strathclyde Passenger Transport system. If only . . . !

A final, personal memory of Waverley Station. During the fine summer of 1940 there was a family holiday at Burntisland which included a day trip to Edinburgh. Duly impressed – I particularly liked the trams in their dignified madder and white livery – we returned to Waverley that evening only to find the train for Burntisland, probably a Thornton local, being announced as 'full and standing' and we joined a group of disconsolate prospective travellers on platform eleven. However, upon instructions from an inspector, the fireman uncoupled the locomotive (an ex-North British 4-4-0, as I recall) which went into the sidings alongside the wall separating the main station from the suburban platforms and then reappeared with an additional coach which was attached to the train and we were comfortably seated for the homeward journey. The fact that this happened during wartime gives a lesson in customer care that Scotrail, the Great North Eastern Railway, Virgin Trains, et al, would do well to learn.

In 1950 a single platform named Easter Road Park Halt was provided on the Leith Central branch for football fans arriving at the Hibernian F.C. ground at Easter Road. This was used for arrivals only, departures following games being from nearby Abbeyhill Station on the Piershill loop. On 15 October 1960 standard class 5 No. 73122 was photographed arriving with a well-filled 12.51 p.m. special from Glasgow Queen Street for a Hibs v Celtic game. By 1967 the halt was disused.

On 15 October 1960 standard class 5 4-6-0 No. 73108 was photographed passing Lochend North Junction as it approached Easter Road Park Halt with a 1.10 p.m. football special from Glasgow Queen Street. This was the second of two trains for a Hibs v Celtic match.

Threat of a new Caledonian suburban line serving Leith resulted in the North British Railway building a massive white elephant in the shape of Leith Central terminal at the foot of Leith Walk. Always under-utilised, it was finally closed to passengers by British Railways in 1952. Five years later it became a diesel maintenance depot and functioned as such until 1972, being demolished in 1989. The short branch from Abbeyhill was traversed by the 'Scottish Rambler' railtour of 19 April 1965 and preserved Great North of Scotland Railway 4-4-0 No. 49, 'Gordon Highlander', is seen outside the erstwhile Leith Central Station, the great roof of which, with an intricate glass screen at the outer end, was a notable feature. No. 49 has been in Glasgow Museum of Transport since 1966.

The Edinburgh & Dalkeith Railway terminus at South Leith was opened in 1838 and, although closed to passengers by the North British Railway at the end of 1904, could be seen until just a few years ago. On 25 August 1962 it was visited by a Stephenson Locomotive Society railtour which is seen here headed by class V3 2-6-2T No. 67668. These were capable locomotives, much used by the London & North Eastern Railway for suburban traffic.

A very typical scene from the Age of Steam, as veteran class J36 0-6-0 No. 65288, built by the North British Railway at their Cowlairs Works in Glasgow in 1897 and rebuilt in 1918, made a brisk departure from South Leith Yard on 15 October 1960, passing Meadows signal box.

The Caledonian's truncated Leith New Lines of 1903 included a substantial, brick-built locomotive shed at Seafield which was soon found to be surplus to requirements. As a result it was let to the North British Railway, while in the Second World War the London & North Eastern Railway used it for an overflow of locomotives from their St Margaret's Depot. On 25 August 1962 class J37 0-6-0 No. 64599 was photographed at the shed which was closed soon after.

Some three years previously, on 7 November 1959, there was considerably more activity at Seafield with J35 0-6-0 No. 64532, J36 0-6-0 No. 65224 (it carried the name 'Mons' in recognition of overseas service in the First World War) and J38 0-6-0 No. 65918 all lined up at the coaling stage.

There was once a well-patronised station at Portobello which opened together with the North British line from Edinburgh to Berwick in June 1846. It was rebuilt some forty years later as an island platform and closed by British Railways in September 1964 under the pretext of ironing out an awkward curve on the east coast main line. On 21 August 1964, class B1 4-6-0 No. 61029, 'Chamois', was photographed as it called with the 4.10 p.m. train from Waverley to Hawick.

Three-quarters of a mile further up the main line was Joppa Station, opened in the very early days of the North British Railway and pictured here on 11 April 1964 with class A3 Pacific No. 60092, 'Fairway', heading the 3.48 p.m. train from Waverley to Berwick. This local service was withdrawn three weeks later and 'Fairway', named after the winner of the 1928 St Leger, went for scrap in October of the same year.

Black Five 4-6-0 No. 45484 passes Portobello East Junction on 16 July 1962 with a Glasgow Fair Holiday excursion train. This ran from Hamilton to Portobello and Waverley, having been routed from Slateford onto the suburban circle line at Craiglockhart and then joining the Waverley Route at Niddrie West Junction.

Of the small branch lines fanning out south of Edinburgh – to Glencorse, Polton and Penicuik – only the first mentioned had a station within the city boundary. This was at Gilmerton, but the passenger service on the branch was withdrawn as early as 1933 although final closure did not come for another sixty years, until the demise of Bilston Glen Colliery at Loanhead. The Stephenson Locomotive Society 'Festival Special' of 29 August 1959 was the last train to traverse the branch in its entirety and is seen here at Gilmerton, headed by preserved North British Railway 4-4-0 No. 256, 'Glen Douglas'. This locomotive can currently be seen in the Scottish Railway Exhibition building at Bo'ness, while Gilmerton figures in 'Line 3' of the proposed City of Edinburgh tram system.

The Niddrie Complex was created as early as 1838 by the Edinburgh & Dalkeith Railway and additions over the years by the North British Railway included the Lothian Lines, which were opened in 1915 to improve access from the Lothian coalfield to Leith docks. On 16 July 1962 class A1 Pacific No. 60147, 'North Eastern', was photographed passing Niddrie West Junction with empty coaches.

Photographed outside the National Coal Board locomotive shed at Niddrie on 20 April 1968 were 0-6-0Ts Nos. 9 and 21, built by Andrew Barclay & Co. Ltd of Kilmarnock in 1911 and 1937 respectively. They were employed shunting a landsale yard, a wagon repair shop and nearby Newcraighall Colliery, as well as a brickworks. No. 9 went new to Arniston Colliery at Gorebridge, not arriving at Niddrie until 1961. No. 21 was delivered to the Niddrie & Benhar Coal Co. and apparently spent all of its working life at Niddrie. Both locomotives were scrapped on site in 1969.

The Stephenson Locomotive Society railtour of 25 August 1962 included, in addition to South Leith, a trip over the St Leonards portion of the Edinburgh & Dalkeith Railway which dated from 1831 and included a tunnel with a one in thirty gradient. For this part of the tour class V3 2-6-2T No. 67668 was replaced by J35 0-6-0 No. 64510. This was the sole survivor of the seventy-six locomotives of this class built by the North British Railway between 1906 and 1913, and in rousing fashion it propelled the train around the foot of Arthur's Seat and up to St Leonards. Back at Duddingston Junction, as the photograph shows, No. 67668 took over for the remainder of the tour, which included the Lothian Lines, Dalkeith and Musselburgh.

Of the stations on the nominally independent – but North British inspired – Edinburgh Suburban & South Side Junction Railway, which opened in 1884, only Newington was of the island platform type. On 19 November 1955 class V3 2-6-2T No. 67606 was photographed arriving with the 1.11 p.m. Outer Circle train from Waverley. The service was dieselised in 1958, but withdrawn in 1962, and several attempts over the past forty years to have it restored have so far been unsuccessful.

Passenger trains on the 'sub', as it was familiarly known, were operated by the North British Railway which added a station at Craiglockhart in 1887. Set in a deep cutting, it is seen here on 14 December 1957 with class D30 4-4-0 No. 62421, 'Laird O' Monkbarns', with the 12.39 p.m. Inner Circle train from Waverley. A connection from Slateford on the former Caledonian main line was opened in 1960.

Saughton Junction, situated three and a half miles north of Waverley Station, is where the line north to the Forth Bridge leaves the former Edinburgh & Glasgow Railway. Completion of the bridge in 1890 brought a massive increase of traffic and resulted in quadrupling of the line from Saughton Junction, together with the rebuilding of Waverley Station. On a wintry 18 January 1964, class V2 2-6-2 No. 60824 was photographed passing Saughton Junction with a 10.55 a.m. relief train from Dundee Tay Bridge.

Photographed on the same day, V2 2-6-2 No. 60818 approaches Saughton Junction from the north with a freight train.

The Edinburgh & Glasgow Railway had a Corstorphine Station (later renamed Saughton and closed in 1921), but a short branch line from Haymarket West Junction, opened by the North British Railway in 1902, provided a convenient terminal in the village. There was also an intermediate station at Pinkhill which, from 1913, served Edinburgh Zoo. Carriage sidings at Corstorphine resulted in a frequent service, but closure came at the end of 1967 despite the branch having obvious potential as a park and ride facility. Class V1 2-6-2T No. 67670 was photographed on 7 September 1954 as it awaited departure with the 6.17 p.m. to Waverley.

Balgreen Halt was opened on the Corstorphine branch, near to its junction with the main line, in 1934 by the London & North Eastern Railway to serve new housing. Class 2MT 2-6-0 No. 46461 was photographed arriving with the 1.38 p.m. from North Berwick to Corstorphine on 12 October 1957. Diesel multiple units took over the service the following year.

On a misty 6 February 1965 class B1 4-6-0 No. 61132, with a ten coach rugby special from Dysart, was photographed passing Haymarket Central Junction and Haymarket Motive Power Depot. The latter had been given over to diesel traction by this date.

The Caledonian Railway completed a goods line from Slateford to Haymarket in 1853 and hoped to reach Leith docks, but the Edinburgh & Glasgow Railway confined them to a bay platform at Haymarket Station. However, for the closure of Princes Street Station the northern end of the spur was revamped as the Duff Street connection. This enabled trains from Glasgow Central and Carstairs to reach Waverley Station and was brought into use in September 1964. On 6 February 1965 Black Five No. 44867, allocated to Stockport Edgeley Shed and fresh from overhaul at Cowlairs Works, was photographed passing with a 1.28 p.m. football special from Waverley to Falkirk Grahamston. The junction is now known as Haymarket East and the spur has been electrified together with the Carstairs line.

Haymarket Station is at the entrance to the tunnel leading to Princes Street Gardens. Its side platforms and centre island platform date from the quadrupling of the tracks in the 1890s, and it retains its impressive Edinburgh & Glasgow Railway terminal building which can be seen behind the locomotive in this view – class B1 4-6-0 No. 61007, 'Klipspringer' (a species of antelope) – as it makes a punctual departure on 12 October 1957 with the 1.20 p.m. train from Waverley to Crail.

On 6 February 1965 class B1 4-6-0 No. 61350 was photographed arriving at Haymarket Station with an 11.50 a.m. special from Hawick for a Scotland v Wales rugby international at Murrayfield.

24

In steam days the four track section to Saughton Junction did not, unfortunately perhaps from the photographic point of view, see many simultaneous departures from Waverley. However, the two departures at four o'clock could provide an exciting spectacle and on 29 August 1955 class A3 Pacific No. 60100, 'Spearmint', bound for Perth, had a head start on A2 Pacific No. 60536, 'Trimbush', which was making for Glasgow.

On a gloomy 26 March 1955 class J83 0-6-0T No. 68481, immaculate in lined black livery, brightened the scene at the west end of Waverley Station. Four of these attractive little locomotives, forty of which had been built at Cowlairs Works in 1900/01, were employed as Waverley pilots for the shunting and marshalling of coaching stock, but were replaced by diesel shunters in 1959. With today's fixed formation trains, station pilots are no longer required.

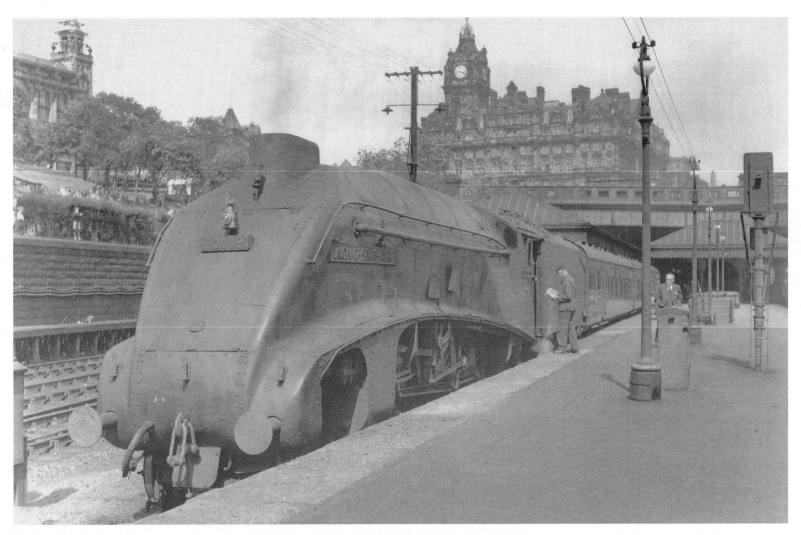

The class A4 Pacifics were synonymous with Waverley Station and No. 60009, 'Union of South Africa', is seen here on 20 July 1959 at platform sixteen, heading the 4.00 p.m. to Perth (via Glenfarg) with through coaches for Inverness. The locomotive has been in private preservation since 1966 and is currently to be found working excursions on the national network, having visited Edinburgh in 2002.

On 7 November 1959 class B1 4-6-0 No. 61148 was captured on film exiting Waverley Station with the 12.30 p.m. train for Dysart.

Five minutes later and No. 61148 was followed by class V3 2-6-2T No. 67615 as it headed the 12.35 p.m. local train for Corstorphine.

Class K4 2-6-0 No. 61998, 'MacLeod of MacLeod', with a Sunday local train for Kirkcaldy, awaits departure from Waverley Station on 12 June 1960. Six of these locomotives were built at the Darlington Works of the London & North Eastern Railway in 1937/38 for use on the West Highland line between Glasgow and Fort William, but ended their days in 1961 working from Thornton Depot in Fife. One has been preserved.

Two express passenger 4-6-2 locomotives had entered service on the Great Northern Railway in 1922 and under the London & North Eastern Railway the class was expanded to a total of seventy-nine. The first to be built by the new company had been named 'Flying Scotsman' and when – as No. 60103 of class A3 – it was withdrawn from service by British Railways in January 1963, it was purchased privately for preservation, restored to apple-green livery, given its original number of 4472 and operated enthusiasts' specials on main lines. In 1969 it was shipped to the USA for several tours of American railroads. Returning in 1973, it is occasionally to be seen hauling railtours (although it is no longer in original condition). On 16 April 1966 it was photographed drawing into platform eleven of Waverley Station punctually at 12.15 p.m. with a special party from Northallerton.

On 16 April 1966 'Mr Pegler's Party' (Alan Pegler was the first owner of No. 4472 in preservation) went forward from Waverley to Inverkeithing, hauled by streamlined Pacific No. 60019, 'Bittern', of the famous A4 class. This locomotive was purchased privately for preservation in September 1966.

Below: At Waverley Station on 4 September 1965 class B1 4-6-0 No. 61344 was photographed awaiting departure from platform sixteen with the 1318 for Crail (the twenty-four hour clock had come into use on British Railways that summer). This formed the last steam train from Edinburgh to the East of Fife line which was closed two days later.

Above: The Caledonian Railway completed their line from Carlisle to Glasgow and Edinburgh in 1848 and firmly established their presence in the capital in 1893 with the opening of a fine new terminal situated at the west end of Princes Street. Preserved Caledonian Railway 4-2-2 No. 123 is pictured here upon arrival on 19 April 1965 with the Easter weekend 'Scottish Rambler' railtour from Glasgow Central. That day the tour ran in two portions, taking in Leith Central (see page 6), St Leonards, Balerno and Carstairs. No. 123 was built by Neilson & Co. of Glasgow in 1886 and went on show at the Edinburgh International Festival the same year, while during the 'Race to Edinburgh' (the competition between the West and East Coast routes) in 1888 it made a record run from Carlisle at an average speed of about sixty miles per hour. Preserved in 1935, it now resides in the Glasgow Museum of Transport.

On the wet autumn evening of 21 October 1963 Black Five No. 45476 was photographed waiting at platform four of Princes Street Station with the 5.18 p.m. for Glasgow Central. Sister engine No. 45214 was at the head of the 5.32 p.m. to Stirling.

The weather was little better on 29 February 1964 when Black Five No. 44978 was photographed leaving Princes Street Station with the 4.22 p.m. train for Perth. The massive signal box housed no less than 156 signal levers which controlled train movements in and around the terminus.

Dalry Road Motive Power Depot was situated three-quarters of a mile from Princes Street Station and was photographed on 29 February 1964 as Black Five No. 44994 passed by with the 12.06 p.m. local train for Kingsknowe. Extravagant motive power indeed for a three coach train on a three mile journey! In addition to Nos. 45360 and 44953, also seen in the photograph, there were fifteen steam locomotives and three diesels in and around the shed that day. The Western Approach Road now occupies the site.

Merchiston Station, a mile and a quarter from Princes Street and opened in 1882, was quickly surrounded by housing as can be seen in this view, taken on 29 February 1964 as Black Five No. 44700 ran in with the 3.05 p.m. from Carstairs to Princes Street.

With the Union Canal aqueduct on the left, Black Five No. 44952 was photographed on 29 February 1964 as it crossed Slateford viaduct with the 2.14 p.m. train from Carstairs which included through coaches from Manchester Victoria.

On 29 February 1964 class 4MT 2-6-4T No. 42273 was photographed arriving at the outer suburban station of Kingsknowe (originally named Slateford) with the 12.57 p.m. from Princes Street. The station closed four months later, but was reopened in 1971. The present Slateford Station was opened in 1853.

Perhaps the most scenic of the Edinburgh branch lines was that to Balerno which formed a six mile loop from Slateford to rejoin the Carstairs line at Ravelrig after traversing the sylvan valley of the Water of Leith and serving several paper mills. Opened in 1874, its passenger service was suspended (never to resume) during the Second World War, although freight traffic continued until 1967 and in the final years there were three special trains for enthusiasts. That of 20 June 1962 is pictured with class 2P 0-4-4T No. 55260 taking water at Currie. After closure, the trackbed was made into a walkway. However, in view of Edinburgh's traffic congestion, a light railway or tramway might well have been a more realistic option.

In 1861 the Caledonian Railway opened a freight line (in conjunction with the Duke of Buccleuch) to Granton Harbour from their Slateford – Haymarket branch and in 1879 began a passenger service to Leith, leaving the Granton line at Crewe Junction. On 12 October 1957 class 3F ex-Caledonian 0-6-0 No. 57550 was photographed near Murrayfield Station with the 1.43 p.m. train from Leith North to Princes Street. The suffix 'North' had been added by British Railways to distinguish the former Caledonian Station at Leith from various other stations there, but this was somewhat confusing as there was a former North British Station (closed to passengers in 1947) named North Leith which now became Leith Citadel!

Despite dieselisation of the Leith North service in 1958, steam trains could be photographed on the occasion of rugby internationals at Murrayfield and cup ties at Tynecastle when steam trains, with their greater seating capacity, were used instead of diesel multiple units. Thus, on 19 March 1960, class J39 0-6-0 No. 64946 steamed out of Dalry Road Station with the 1.40 p.m. from Princes Street to Leith North. Despite its cramped site alongside the motive power depot, the station at Dalry Road had a wide island platform and was situated between Dalry Junction on the Carstairs line and Dalry Middle Junction where the Leith North branch and the Wester Dalry spur to Haymarket West Junction parted company.

On 19 March 1960 former Caledonian Railway '812' class 0-6-0 No. 57565 was photographed passing Dalry Middle Junction with the 1.37 p.m. train from Leith North to Edinburgh Princes Street.

Trains from Leith to Edinburgh left the Granton line at Coltbridge Junction, seen here on 19 March 1960 with class J39 0-6-0 No. 64986 heading the 2.10 p.m. from Leith North to Princes Street. The spur diverging in the foreground joined the line to Slateford at Granton Junction.

The running of dining car specials from Glasgow Central direct to Murrayfield Station on the occasion of rugby internationals dated back to Caledonian Railway days. These trains, loading to ten or more vehicles and double headed, used the line from Slateford to Coltbridge Junction, as seen here on 19 March 1960 with standard class 5MT 4-6-0s Nos. 73060 and 73076 hauling a 12.40 p.m. special from Glasgow. A second train at 12.56 p.m. from Glasgow was worked by Nos. 73062 and 73063.

Standard Fives Nos. 73076 and 73075, photographed on 23 February 1963 approaching Coltbridge Junction soon after leaving Murrayfield Station with a 5.20 p.m. dining car excursion returning to Glasgow Central. The provision of locomotives with consecutive numbers had been something of a tradition at Glasgow's Polmadie shed for these trains, but this was the last occasion on which steam power was used.

The uncompleted Leith New Lines of the Caledonian Railway included a line from Newhaven, on their existing Leith branch, to a new terminus at Leith East. This was used only for freight traffic and proposed passenger stations were never completed. These would have included platforms at Newhaven to connect with the existing station, as seen in this photograph (the overgrown platform is to the right of the train) taken on 7 November 1959 with class J39 0-6-0 No. 64986 on the 2.10 p.m. from Leith North to Princes Street. The normal diesel multiple units had been replaced by a steam train which was advertised as a football special to Dalry Road Station for a Hearts home game at Tynecastle Stadium.

Leith North terminus was a Spartan affair with an island platform and a rudimentary wooden train shed which, surprisingly, still exists (for industrial purposes) and is very conveniently sited for both the Ocean Terminal shopping centre and extensive new housing. Unfortunately, the trains ceased to run in 1962! This photograph was taken on 30 September 1961 and shows former Caledonian Railway 0-4-4T No. 55124 about to leave with a Branch Line Society railtour.

Prior to the opening of the Slateford – Craiglockhart connection in 1960, the main interchange point for freight traffic between the former Caledonian and North British systems in Edinburgh was at Granton Harbour. In this photograph class J37 0-6-0 No. 64594 is seen on one such train on 7 April 1958.